Animals in My Backyard

BADGERS

Aaron Carr

www.av2books.com

AV² provides enriched content that supplements and complements this book. Weigl's AV² books strive to create inspired learning and engage young minds in a total learning experience.

Your AV² Media Enhanced books come alive with...

Go to **www.av2books.com,** and enter this book's unique code.

BOOK CODE

Q355602

AV² by Weigl brings you media enhanced books that support active learning.

Audio
Listen to sections of the book read aloud.

Video
Watch informative video clips.

Embedded Weblinks
Gain additional information for research.

Try This!
Complete activities and hands-on experiments.

Key Words
Study vocabulary, and complete a matching word activity.

Quizzes
Test your knowledge.

Slide Show
View images and captions, and prepare a presentation.

... and much, much more!

Published by AV² by Weigl.
350 5th Avenue, 59th Floor New York, NY 10118
Websites: www.av2books.com www.weigl.com

Library of Congress Control Number: 2013953032

ISBN 978-1-4896-0536-8 (hardcover)
ISBN 978-1-4896-0537-5 (softcover)
ISBN 978-1-4896-0538-2 (single-user eBook)
ISBN 978-1-4896-0539-9 (multi-user eBook)

Printed in the United States of America in North Mankato, Minnesota
1 2 3 4 5 6 7 8 9 0 17 16 15 14 13

122013
WEP301113

Project Coordinator: Aaron Carr   Designer: Mandy Christiansen

Weigl acknowledges Getty Images as the primary image supplier for this title.

Animals in My Backyard
BADGERS

CONTENTS

Meet the badger.

He is a small animal with a striped face.

When he was young,
he lived with his mother.

With his mother, he stayed safe
and learned how to find food.

He has very sharp claws.

With his very sharp claws,
he can dig in the ground.

He can make a strong smell.

By making a strong smell,
he can keep himself safe.

He has a very good sense of smell.

His very good sense of smell helps him find food.

He looks for food
by digging in the ground.

By digging in the ground,
he finds small animals and bugs to eat.

He lives in a hole in the ground.

This hole in the ground
is called a sett.

17

He sleeps during the day.

Sleeping during the day
lets him look for food at night.

If you meet the badger,
he may be surprised.
He might run at you.

If you meet the badger,
stay back.

20

BADGER FACTS

These pages provide more detail about the interesting facts found in the book. They are intended to be used by adults as a learning support to help young readers round out their knowledge of each animal featured in the *Animals in My Backyard* series.

Pages 4–5

Badgers are small animals with striped faces. They are short and stocky with strong legs and distinctive coloring. There are 10 species of badger, each with slight differences in coloring. Most badgers have at least one white stripe on the face or head. Badgers are part of the weasel family. They are usually about 9 inches (23 centimeters) tall, 30 inches (76 cm) long, and weigh about 26 pounds (12 kilograms).

Pages 6–7

Badgers live with their mothers when they are young. Females may give birth to between one and five babies, or cubs, at once. Cubs are born with their eyes closed. They open their eyes after about five weeks. By eight weeks, they are ready to begin learning to find food with their mother. Badgers reach full size after just six months, but they are not ready to live on their own until they are about two years old.

Pages 8–9

Badgers have very sharp claws. They use their claws to help them dig in the ground. A badger's claws can be up to 2 inches (5 cm) long. These long claws are only on the larger front paws, though. The smaller back paws have shorter claws. This is because badgers use their front claws for digging.

Pages 10–11

Badgers can release a strong scent. They use this foul-smelling scent to scare other animals away. This is similar to a skunk spraying a smelly liquid to scare predators away. Unlike skunks, though, badgers cannot spray their scent. Instead, they release the scent where they stand, like a stink bomb.

Pages 12–13

Badgers have a very good sense of smell. They have poor eyesight, so badgers rely on smell to help them do most of their daily activities. Badgers use smell to find food, identify members of their group, spot intruders from other groups, recognize danger, and find their way around. Some scientists have suggested that the badger's sense of smell may be up to 800 times stronger than a human's.

Pages 14–15

Badgers look for food by digging in the ground. They find most of their food underground. Badgers are classified as carnivores, or meat eaters, but many species eat plants as well. American badgers mostly eat small animals, such as rodents and snakes. These animals hide underground, so badgers dig quickly to catch their food.

Pages 16–17

Badgers live in holes in the ground. These holes are called setts. Parts of a sett can be 30 feet (9 meters) underground. Some badgers live alone, but most badgers live in groups called clans. A clan lives together in a large sett with many tunnels and rooms. Badgers prefer grassland and forest areas. The American badger is found in open areas such as prairies and along the edges of wooded areas.

Pages 18–19

Badgers sleep during the day. They are nocturnal. This means they sleep during the day and are active at night. Badgers sleep in nesting areas inside their setts. Some badgers that live alone dig a new sett each night before going to sleep. When they leave these setts, other animals may move in and use them as homes.

Pages 20–21

Beware of badgers when in nature. People do not often see badgers in their natural habitat. This is because badgers only come out at night, and they can usually smell people coming from far away. If people do encounter badgers in nature, it is best to stay away. If a badger gets scared, it may hiss, growl, and bare its teeth. Keep a safe distance from the badger and avoid making any sudden movements.

KEY WORDS

Research has shown that as much as 65 percent of all written material published in English is made up of 300 words. These 300 words cannot be taught using pictures or learned by sounding them out. They must be recognized by sight. This book contains 45 common sight words to help young readers improve their reading fluency and comprehension. This book also teaches young readers several important content words. These words are paired with pictures to aid in learning and improve understanding.

Page	Sight Words First Appearance
4	the
5	a, animal, face, he, is, small, with
6	and, find, food, his, how, lived, mother, to, was, when, young
8	has, very
9	can, in
10	make
11	by, keep
12	good, of
13	helps, him
14	for, looks
15	eat
16	this
18	day
19	at, lets, night
20	back, be, if, may, might, run, you

Page	Content Words First Appearance
4	badger
8	claws
9	ground
10	smell
12	sense
15	bugs
16	hole, sett